JUMPSTARTS!

ALSO BY EARMA BROWN

Write Your Best Book Now! (Paperback)
How to Write a Book In 100 Days (Paperback)
Self Publishing Your Way Now (Paperback)
40+ Article Writing Templates (Paperback)
Article Marketing Speedway (eBook)
eBook it! (eBook)

Visit http://butterflypress.net/store/

JUMPSTARTS

100 Book Writing Tips, Exercises and Quotable Encouragement

Earma Brown

Butterfly Press
Dallas, Texas

JUMPSTARTS

TABLE OF CONTENTS

INTRODUCTION

Have you started your book yet? No. Don't think about it any longer. You know the words; now say it with me. Just do it! With the right focus and information, you can successfully begin, complete and even publish YOUR book within a few months this year.

More and more people are successfully completing their books in less time. Even your competitors are getting it done. Why not join them? Here's 100 tips, action steps and quotable encouragement to JUMP start writing your book now. Inside this book you will discover tips on how to:

- Create your book's thesis
- Write the easy way to sell sooner
- Make an inspiration cover early
- Write compelling copy
- Make your mark in the world
- Stamp pro on your book
- Find your writing rhythm
- Use laser focus

Don't put it off any longer. Take your dream off the waiting list. If you continue to wait, you can be this time next year without making your dream of writing a successful book come true. You have the plan, the knowledge and the solution. Now write it all down in a book. Your audience is waiting. Stop giving in to procrastination; implement the tips inside this book and write a book that sells well. Make it different. Make it count. Make it yours.

To your success,

Earma Brown

JUMPSTART: TIP 1

Our goals can only be reached through a vehicle of a plan, in which we must fervently believe, and upon which we must vigorously act. There is no other route to success. —Stephen A. Brennan

PLAN A SHORT BOOK FIRST.

Many aspiring writers overwhelm themselves with goals of a 365 page book first. Shorten your book to 25-90 pages the first time or divide your large book into a smaller book one and two. Even consider an ebook to test the market.

Whatever you decide, though you shorten it, still fill it with useful information by using the question and answer format for each chapter. Using the same format and length for each chapter and answering all your readers' questions will not only speed your writing process but it will result in a successful book.

ACTION STEP:

Set a shorter goal. Decide if your longer project can be shortened by doing it in two volumes or a shorter version. For example, a client of mine divided her 300 plus page non-fiction volume into two 150-page books. Now, take some pressure off yourself; revise your goal accordingly and get it done. Write your goal on next page:

NOTES

JUMPSTART: TIP 2

A professional writer is an amateur who didn't quit. —*Richard Bach*

USE TECHNOLOGY TO LEVERAGE SUCCESS

Successful writers embrace technology. They discover how to use their word processing software more efficiently saving time on getting their book to market.

They learn to use new marketing techniques that will multiply and expand their profit streams by as much as eight times. They use their websites and email lists to build their brand name, create more product awareness, follow up on their customers and leverage their profits.

ACTION STEP:

Discover how to use the short-cut steps of your favorite word processing software. Take a course; pull out your manual; buy a cheat sheet. Whatever you do learn how to use your software more effectively.

NOTES

_____

_____

_____

_____

_____

_____

_____

_____

_____

_____

_____

_____

_____

JUMPSTART: TIP 3

Write well but above all write passionately! –Earma Brown

SETUP PASSION POINTS TO GUIDE YOUR BOOK TO SUCCESS.

Every part of your book should be written passionately and designed to be a sales tool. Touch your readers' emotion with passion for your topic and you'll sell more books. In fact, when you design your book to include passion points, you'll sell more books than you ever imagined.

Include these passion points and prosper: Write to help one targeted audience, Sizzle your title & book cover, Develop one central thought per book, Make it unique, Design a mini-billboard, Write your back cover before you write your book, Develop your book introduction, Make a table of contents, Sizzle all chapter titles & headings, and Contact influencers of your field.

ACTION STEP:

Pull out a sheet of paper or on the note page in this book; number one through nine. List the passion points for your book. Need help with the passion points for your book? Sign up for the **100 Days** book writing course at http://bookwritingcourse.com or get a copy of *Write Your Best Book Now* book and/or same name course book for detailed help.

NOTES

_____

_____

_____

_____

_____

_____

_____

_____

_____

_____

_____

_____

JUMPSTART: TIP 4

Success is the ability to go from failure to failure without losing your enthusiasm. —Winston Churchill

SIZZLE YOUR TITLE AND BOOK COVER.

Remember, your title may well be 90% of the magnetic pulling power for your book. Researchers say you have approximately 4 seconds to hook your potential buyer. An excellent title is short. The top titles are benefit driven. Don't forget to heat them up with emotion. Use terms your audience can relate to.

Use action words and verbs. Quantify change with ways and time limits. Use one or two word ideas to tell a story. Pledge change. Spark interest. Instead of How *to Write an E-book* the author chose the title *Ten Secrets to Write Your E-book Like a Winner*. She quantified change, sparked interest and branded her title.

ACTION STEP:

Develop a working title for your book or next book. Implement the principles above for a sizzling title. Write at least 3 title ideas on the note page. Need extra help with crafting your sizzling title? Use the Book Title Tutorial at **http://butterflypress.net/store/**

NOTES

JUMPSTART: TIP 5

There is no rule on how to write. Sometimes it comes easily and perfectly;
sometimes it's like drilling rock and then blasting it out with charges.
—Ernest Hemingway

MINE YOUR KNOWLEDGE LIKE GOLD.

One of the main concepts of the 7 step writing program of the *Write Your Best Book Now* book includes excavating your unique groups of existing knowledge and opinions. Many people think they have to be super smart while doing tons of research on a topic they barely know anything about much less feel any passion for.

Following this program you will put out modules or nuggets from existing information from your speeches, classes, articles, brochures. If you've never done this before, you may be surprised at what turns up.

When you organize your information into groups and categories, it will be easier to write your book and easier to repackage your ideas into newsletters, articles, speeches and website reports that will help market and sell your book.

ACTION STEP:

Over the next few days, pull out all of the existing information related to your book topic. Begin to organize this information into topics. Write below at least 3 groups of information that you will pull from. For example, start with your career, hobby and/or extra research. Begin a topic list on your note page inside this book.

NOTES

_____

_____

_____

_____

_____

_____

_____

_____

_____

_____

_____

_____

JUMPSTART: TIP 6

Writing is an exploration. You start from nothing and learn as you go.
—E. L. Doctorow

MORE ABOUT MINING THE GOLD CALLED YOUR KNOWLEDGE!
Re-examine the files full of your writing and speaking. Even if you are not published yet, you probably have a lot more knowledge stored that you have written or created than you realize. As a professional, you have written memos, proposals and reports. You may have conducted meetings, delivered presentations and speeches or short talks. These may all contain valuable information which you have forgotten.

Make another list and write down the title or topic of every article, proposal, report or presentation that you have ever given. Next to the topic or title write down the main idea that you developed in them.

Then skim the actual report, speech or article and look for relevant nuggets of information that you can re-use. Dissect each piece for ideas that should be added to your topic.

ACTION STEP:

Organize all of the information you pulled out. Include the notes you jotted down for your book. If not already, start below your list of topics you found.

NOTES

_____

_____

_____

_____

_____

_____

_____

_____

_____

_____

_____

_____

_____

JUMPSTART: TIP 7

Your decision to be, have and do something out of ordinary entails facing difficulties that are out of the ordinary as well. Sometimes your greatest asset is simply your ability to stay with it longer than anyone else. —Brian Tracy

WRITING A BOOK IS A JOURNEY.

Most journeys go so much smoother with a system in place. Take simple steps. Get started fast and gain momentum. Then keep going to completion. Start today; complete and release your significant message to the world. Value your time. Learn how to do what you already know easier and faster.

Many people say, "I don't know anything about computers so pecking my book out would probably take forever." Stop making excuses. Don't run from technology. At least take the time to learn about the shortcuts in your current software. Welcome to the new millennium! Embrace technology make your software work efficiently for you.

ACTION STEP:

Repeat after me, "I will not allow my lack of knowledge to stop me from pursuing my dream this year. I will not excuse myself for any reason from getting started this week."(Looking for an organized plan? Try the book writing course at **http://bookwritingcourse.com** for a 12 step book writing plan.)

NOTES

_____

_____

_____

_____

_____

_____

_____

_____

_____

_____

_____

_____

JUMPSTART: TIP 8

Personally, I'm always ready to learn, although I do not always like being taught. —*Winston Churchill*

CREATE A FABULOUS FRAMEWORK TO HOUSE EACH CHAPTER.

In my opinion, the best non-fiction books have a set structure to house their chapters. That structure provides the framework for each chapter. It's stressful to re-invent the wheel every time with a blank screen.

Most people including the author are intimidated by a blank screen. Instead of starting from scratch each chapter, use repeating elements to create structure. In John Maxwell's *21 Irrefutable Laws of Leadership: Follow Them and People Will Follow You* foreword by Zig Ziglar contains repeating elements that house each chapter. Each chapter has the same basic form.

ACTION STEP:

Write a list (start with 7-10) of questions about your book topic. Now take them one by one and answer them. When you begin writing your book, take this list of questions and answers and expound on each to create your chapters.

NOTES

_____

_____

_____

_____

_____

_____

_____

_____

_____

_____

_____

_____

JUMPSTART: TIP 09

Ideas shape the course of history. —*John Maynard Keynes*

CREATE FRAMEWORK FOR ORGANIZING YOUR IDEAS

For a short book, simply create a list of every idea related to your book's topic. Once you start your list and create a structure you'll be surprised at how quickly your book takes shape.

Now take your list and number them in order of importance. After your ideas have been prioritized, you can easily spot patterns of what will lead to writing a book on what you are most passionate about.

ACTION STEP:

Create a list of every idea related to your book's topic; then create a structure.

NOTES

_____

_____

_____

_____

_____

_____

_____

_____

_____

_____

_____

_____

JUMPSTART: TIP 10

When you have an important point to make, don't try to be subtle or clever. Use a pile driver. Hit the point once. Then come back and hit it again. Then hit it a third time— a tremendous whack. — Winston Churchill

DEVELOP ONE CENTRAL THOUGHT PER BOOK

Focus on one topic in your book. It's a known fact bestsellers focus on one main topic. Focus on one topic then write each chapter to support that subject.

When you overload your reader with information, you come across as disorganized, wordy and flat. Instead of including everything you know, stick to one how-to subject and include plenty of simple details with examples to make it useful to your reader.

ACTION STEP:

Write your book's thesis into one or two sentences. Don't forget most bestsellers have one central thought per book.

NOTES

_____

_____

_____

_____

_____

_____

_____

_____

_____

_____

_____

_____

JUMPSTART: TIP 11

Take a chance! All life is a chance. The man who goes the furthest is generally the one who is willing to do and dare. —Dale Carnegie

DON'T BE AFRAID TO BRAND

You may have heard as I have, branding is for the big guys ONLY. After all, they have the power and money to make their brand stick in the minds of people. My response is: did they (the big guys) all start out with non-descript cookie cutter ideas? Or did they start with small unique ideas and big passion?

My point is, go ahead make it unique, make it special, and make it your own. Remember the acronym and term 'your USP – Unique Selling Proposition' that most marketers teach and swear by. Well, a little twist on that for your book, "Make your message stand out with your own unique selling point." Don't copy. You can still use your successful mentor's work as a guideline but come up with your own take on a common subject.

Brand yourself, your business and your book. <u>Think about the greatest benefit that you offer through your book or service.</u> Consider your book and chapter titles. Now think about your keywords and headings on your website. Do you see a repeating word that stands out?

For example, the book "Write Your Best Book Now" the author threads some form of "win" throughout her materials. Ever heard of the Chicken Soup for the Soul series? The title changes with each audience but the Chicken Soup brand stays the same. For example, there's a Chicken Soup for Teen-agers, Chicken Soup for Mothers, Chicken Soup for Prisoners and so on.

ACTION STEP:

List top three things you are passionate about. Remember your passion will help carry you through the work and as with any worthwhile project-challenges:

NOTES

_____

_____

_____

_____

_____

_____

_____

_____

_____

_____

_____

_____

_____

JUMPSTART: TIP 12

Don't reinvent the wheel, just realign it. —Anthony J. D'Angelo

AVOID RE-INVENTING THE WHEEL.

Use the information you already have. Your audience is looking for solutions to their problems. They are looking to you for encouragement to overcome their challenges.

Mine your background, your files, and your speeches for the gold called your knowledge. Use speedy book writing techniques and finish your book faster to sell sooner. Stay with what you know.

You're the expert. To have the best chance to get your book done in the next 100 days, use what you have already written. Use your speeches, your seminars, your notes and experiences. Fill your book with your stories, case studies and examples.

ACTION STEP:

Examine your files for existing information you can use in your book. Record what blocks of information you discover on the next page.

NOTES

_____

_____

_____

_____

_____

_____

_____

_____

_____

_____

_____

_____

JUMPSTART: TIP 13

Do not wait; the time will never be "just right." Start where you stand, and work with whatever tools you may have at your command, and better tools will be found as you go along. —Napoleon Hill

ENGAGE YOUR READER

Include engagement tools in your chapters. You add value and interest by including several engagement tools. Sprinkle interesting ways for your reader to interact with your material. For example, include worksheets, note sheets and lists to engage your readers and make them an active participant.

Your engagement tool can be as simple as a set of review questions at the end of each chapter to encourage thoughtful reflections of the points covered in the chapter. Or consider how this book is setup with action steps outlined designed to help the reader take action on each principle.

Checklist and worksheets are the two most common engagement tools. Checklists provide a framework for readers to answer questions, define their goals and identify available resources. Worksheets also help readers measure their progress with applying the principles in your book.

ACTION STEP:

Make a list of engagement tools you can use in your book. Will the end-of-the-chapter questions engage your reader best? Or should you include a list of review questions to prompt thought and reflection?

NOTES

_____

_____

_____

_____

_____

_____

_____

_____

_____

_____

_____

JUMPSTART: TIP 14

You are never really playing against an opponent. You are playing against yourself, your own highest standards. And when you reach your limit that is real joy. —Arthur Ashe

GET ORGANIZED!

Researchers say we waste over 150 hours a year looking for mislaid information. Develop an organization method that fits you.

For example, to save time and get organized you can create a master folder with your book's title. Inside, keep a separate file for each chapter. Assign each chapter a short title that will make sense later. If you don't have a title then assign names by topic. Put research notes or resources in each chapter named folder.

For longer books, create a separate folder for your book and each chapter. Create a hard copy file folder and a computer folder in your directory list. In Microsoft Word select 'Save As' under File. Go to *My Documents* and create a folder name after your book.

Put all your book related files in this folder. For shorter version books, make sure you create a separate folder for your book so you can easily find it when you are ready to work.

ACTION STEP:

Get organized to get rid of time-wasters. Write your organization plan below. Better yet, if you have some time, just do it, get started now. If not, set aside an hour or two to organize your files and/or purchase a file cabinet, folders and labels for your book project:

NOTES

JUMPSTART: TIP 15

Something in human nature causes us to start slacking off at our moment of greatest accomplishment. As you become successful, you will need a great deal of self-discipline not to lose your sense of balance, humility, and commitment.
—*Ross Perot*

FINISH FAST & FINISH STRONG!

I know everyone is different. So what works for me may be different than what works for you. But here's an idea I and many others have used successfully over and over again.

Create a Chapter Template

After you have outlined or structured your book with the repeating elements in each chapter, create a template which will form the basis of each chapter.

For longer books, you should create a separate template file named after each chapter. i.e. "03 chapter passion points." For shorter books, I just create separate pages for each chapter.

After creating the template file or page, go through and insert placeholder text for each element of the chapter. For example, the chapter template for one of my books looked like this:

Chapter Number	Chapter Title
Quote	Introduction
Principle 1	Principle 2
Principle 3...	Conclusion

ACTION STEP:

If not already, create your chapter template. Develop your chapter format. For example, each chapter will have a chapter title, quote (interesting fact), introduction, main point or solution, supporting facts, summary or provocative questions and end of chapter.

NOTES

_____

_____

_____

_____

_____

_____

_____

_____

_____

_____

_____

_____

_____

JUMPSTART: TIP 16

Twenty years from now you will be more disappointed by the things you didn't do than by the ones you did. So throw off the bowlines. Sail away from the safe harbor. Catch the trade winds in your sails. Explore. Dream. Discover.
—Mark Twain

DO IT NOW FOR NOW IS BETTER THAN LATER.

Act now. Too many of us for too long have hid behind the words, "It's too hard." Now is the time to take charge of our fears and conquer them. First things first, to overcome procrastination -the fear of failure- is to act now. Most times the bottom line of procrastination is fear of failure.

Remember, action will destroy fear. Each successful step of your system will deal a death blow to fear.

ACTION STEP:

Select <u>step one</u> of a writing program and begin today. Sign-up for twelve lesson online course at http://100daystoabook.com or if getting started is still overwhelming consider the FREE mini-course *Jumpstart Your Book* at http://writetowin.org/jumpstartyourbook.htm Or take the Seven Day Challenge at **http://writeabookchallenge.com** Write your commitment on the next page.

NOTES

_____

_____

_____

_____

_____

_____

_____

_____

_____

_____

_____

_____

_____

_____

_____

JUMPSTART: TIP 17

"Writing is easy: All you do is sit staring at a blank sheet of paper until drops of blood form on your forehead." —Gene Fowler

TITLE MINI-TUTORIAL, PART I

Now is a good time to spark interest and now is a good time to develop your title/headline writing skill. You can use it to title your book well. Is your book title already written? No worries, you'll need this skill to headline your articles, your web site, your brochures, ads and the list could go on.

An excellent way to develop an engaging title is to arouse your prospective reader's curiosity. Tease their curiosity and they will pick it up then buy it to find out what it's about. The infamous "Who Move My Cheese: An amazing way to deal with change in your work and in your life" by Spencer Johnson had a curious title that moved millions to buy.

It stayed on the best seller list for 5+ years selling more than 14 million copies in 40 different languages. If the same book had been titled something like, "How to Deal with Change in Your Work and Your Life", few people would have been curious. But the Who Moved My Cheese teased readers with an invitation to read or at least pick it up.

Another curiosity title is Rich Dad, Poor Dad: What the Rich Teach Their Kids About Money – that the Poor and Middle Class Do Not! by Robert Kiyosaki and Sharon L. Lechter. The title instantly engages your curiosity with the question, "What would I know if my dad was rich?"

ACTION STEP:

Do a rough draft of your chapter titles. If you haven't gotten this far, consider writing eight to ten questions your book will answer. Group and categorize the questions. Now re-list them assigning a catchy title to each. Voila! You have a rough draft of your chapter titles and table of contents.

NOTES

JUMPSTART: TIP 18

When people are highly motivated, it's easy to accomplish the impossible. And when they're not, it's impossible to accomplish the easy. —*Bob Collings*

Title Mini-Tutorial, part II

Now is a good time to develop your title/headline writing skill. Quantify change and add time limits. You can use it to title your book well. Is your book title already set in stone? No worries, you'll need this skill to headline your articles, your web site, your brochures, ads and the list could go on.

A good characteristic to use in developing your best title is to promise change. In your title spell out the change that readers can expect if they follow your book's precepts. Let them know what to expect. Use steps, ways and time limits to promise change.

You can add focus and credibility to your title by adding a time frame or quantifying change. C.J. Hayden's book "Get Clients Now!: A 28-Day Marketing Program for Professionals and Consultants" The first part of the title tells what the book is about. Adding now brings immediacy. The (28-Day) part emphasizes that the reader will get day-by-day instruction and probably enjoys results in less than a month.

Other good examples of quantifying change are "The 7 Habits of Highly Effective People" by Stephen R. Covey and "7 Steps to Fearless Speaking" by Lilyan Wilder.

Another change oriented title is "Weigh Down: An Inspirational Way to Lose Weight, Stay Slim and Find a New You" or "How to Be a Great Communicator In Person, On Paper, and on the Podium: The Complete System for communication Effectively in Business & In Life.

Change motivating titles often begin by identifying their target market including the problem, event or characteristics the book address. In doing so, they promise an easy structure leading to the promised change. List instantly communicate easier success by changing big task into a series of smaller tasks.

ACTION STEP:

Develop your book's working title. Your title will become your hook for your book once finished. But for now whatever stirs and motivates <u>you</u> will be good.

NOTES

_____

_____

_____

_____

_____

_____

_____

_____

_____

_____

_____

_____

_____

_____

_____

JUMPSTART: TIP 19

Think about your future possibilities and the fact that your potential is virtually unlimited. You can do what you want to do and go where you want to go. You can be the person you want to be. You can set large and small goals and make plans and move step-by-step, progressively toward their realization. There are no obstacles to what you can accomplish except the obstacles that you create in your mind. —Brian Tracy

EXCAVATE YOUR BACKGROUND

Looking for book ideas, article ideas? Don't forget to mine your background. As you look for ideas, don't leave out reviewing your work history and/or volunteer history and create another list. Note any boards you have served on.

Examine the associations and organizations you have been a member of over the years. Organize this one by employer, client, and organization. Examine every job, client and task. Think about things you learned.

What mistakes did you observe? What procedures did you learn? What were the pros and cons of the relationship? Examine all successes and failures. What were any lessons learned? Make a note of what you feel you gained from each experience with a job, client or organization.

ACTION STEP:

Write your book's introduction including why you wrote your book, how it will benefit your reader and a short explanation of the format of your book.

NOTES

_____

_____

_____

_____

_____

_____

_____

_____

_____

_____

_____

_____

_____

_____

_____

JUMPSTART: TIP 20

I have heard it said that the first ingredient of success - the earliest spark in the dreaming youth - is this: dream a great dream. —*John A. Appleman*

CREATE A SYSTEM

The process of checking your background for ideas should be continuous. As you write your book, you will find yourself continuing the process of organizing and re-organizing your ideas. Take your list of ideas and add any nuggets you located while reviewing your background, speeches and articles.

As you progress, new ideas will come to you. It's o.k. to jot your ideas down on a piece of paper until you have a chance to file it. But for some of us, our desk can quickly become a hodge-podge of stickys and scraps of paper. Now is the time to create your a system that you will use throughout writing your book. Judy Cullins puts it like this, "Stop Piling and Start Filing."

<u>Research experts say over 150 hours a year is wasted looking for misplaced paper.</u> Organization is key because the Pareto Time Management says that only 10% of our papers are actually important.

ACTION STEP:

Stop! Are you as organized as you could be? No. Then take a moment to do this: file everything that's on your desk. Do you have too much to do at this moment? Consider scheduling a filing day. Or better yet, delegate this task to your helper or assistant. For now write your to-do list for this week on the next page.

NOTES

JUMPSTART: TIP 21

No one lives long enough to learn everything they need to learn starting from scratch. To be successful, we absolutely, positively have to find people who have already paid the price to learn the things that we need to learn to achieve our goals. —Brian Tracy

LEARN TO DELEGATE AND SHARE FASTER AND FASTER

Don't succumb to the feeling that you have to do it all yourself. As writers, we can get pretty isolated in our thinking if we're not careful. Do your research and reading time apart from your writing sessions. You may be able to ask your spouse, a teen-aged son or daughter, a friend to help with your research.

Know when to let go of your chapters and book. Don't self-edit and pick your book apart word by word. Learn to use your skills at the highest level possible. Some of the mechanical tasks of proofreading ask a family member, part-time employee or again a friend to help. After you have done the best job you can with your manuscript, don't be afraid to pass it to a professional. Learn to delegate faster and faster.

ACTION STEP:

Choose your book's title or select a chapter and its headings. Revise them until they sizzle like bacon frying in a skillet. Are you a vegetarian? O.k., sizzle them like a Fourth of July rocket. Then let go.

NOTES

JUMPSTART: TIP 22

Most people are so busy knocking themselves out trying to do everything they think they should do, they never get around to what they want to do.
—Kathleen Winsor

REWRITE AND REVISE

Successful authors rewrite and organize their ideas for the most impact. New authors tell me all the time, "I just write whatever comes to my head and there's no need to re-write. My editor will handle all that."

My response is always the same: It's o.k. to free write when you are working on your first draft. The idea is to get the thoughts out of your head onto paper. For no one can express it quite like you. Oh sure, there are some better or worse writers but not exactly like you.

In fact, my advice is to avoid re-writing during your first draft. Concentrate on finishing each chapter then use your tracking time to self-edit: Check your ideas for flow, grammar, spelling, and chapter endings. Work on your chapter titles and lead in introductions.

I know this may not feel good to some but its smacks of plain laziness if you don't work on making your copy the best it can be. Don't leave all the dirty work for your editor unless you really can't do any better.

ACTION STEP:

Choose your favorite chapter that you have written in your book so far. Revise it and write a stronger lead. You can practice on the note sheet inside this book.

NOTES

_____

_____

_____

_____

_____

_____

_____

_____

_____

_____

_____

_____

_____

_____

_____

JUMPSTART: TIP 23

Every great work, every big accomplishment, has been brought into manifestation through holding to the vision, and often just before the big achievement, comes apparent failure and discouragement.
—Florence Scovel Shinn

SET YOURSELF UP FOR SUCCESS

Use the tracking approach. I can't keep up with where I am after interruptions of life. It is a common challenge to find your place after being interrupted with family, work and daily life.

After all that's why many think you must get away to get it done effectively. Yet, there's hope for those who can't get away or choose not to. Successful writers all over the world use the tracking approach. They succeed because they commit to doing a little each day.

Time is a method where you commit to a writing a certain amount of time each day. With the cumulative factor involved your commitment doesn't have to be that much.

For example, to accomplish my book writing goals I commit to writing one hour a day in my most productive time. With this method don't be overly concerned about how much you write, just keep the time commitment.

Another method is focused on output. Commit to writing a certain number of words or pages a day, perhaps 750-1,000 words or approximately 3 ½ pages double-spaced text. The key factor is to stick to it until completion.

ACTION STEP:

Choose a method to track your work; briefly explain why you chose this method and write it below.

NOTES

_____

_____

_____

_____

_____

_____

_____

_____

_____

_____

_____

_____

_____

_____

_____

JUMPSTART: TIP 24

Success demands focus. It is the hallmark of all truly great people. Your ability to get and remain focused or lack thereof is perhaps the key determinant of your success. —*Gary Ryan Blair*

AVOID MARATHON WRITING.

Have you thought, "I have to get away from everything to write a successful book?" No you don't.

I know several novelist and non-fiction book writers who had to write during a long commute to get their best book written and out to the world.

They accomplished it because they systematically worked on their book until it was done. In the midst of your busy life, designate your time to write (work on your book) with a goal to completion. (reasonable time to completion)

ACTION STEP:

Choose your designated time to write. Write it down in your note section as an intention goal. For example, I write every day at 10:00 pm for at least one hour except Sundays until my book is done.

NOTES

JUMPSTART: TIP 25

To write what is worth publishing, to find honest people to publish it, and get sensible people to read it, are the three great difficulties in being an author.
—Charles Caleb Colton

WRITE TO HELP ONE TARGETED AUDIENCE.

It's true not everyone wants your book. But there is a community of people in your field waiting for you to solve their problem. What problems does your message solve for them?

Develop an audience profile (picture) and keep it in front of you as you write. That way you can visualize a real person to solve problems for. Though 78% market is women who buy books, choosing an audience of women is not narrow enough.

Chicken Soup for Mothers, Chicken Soup for the Teenager, for the Prisoner and other specific groups sold way more copies than the original Chicken Soup.

ACTION STEP:

Develop an audience profile for your book. For example, I visualized and described my writer friend (a real person) that needed the steps to write a book.

NOTES

JUMPSTART: TIP 26

Don't tell me the moon is shining; show me the glint of light on broken glass.
—Anton Chekhov

DESIGN A 30 SECOND POSTER BOARD.

Sprinkle this poster board throughout your book, your speeches, elevator conversation, radio spots. Let your passion for your topic shine for a few seconds in this poster board.

After all, you only have a few seconds to make an impression on the media, the agent, the bookseller, the individual buyer. Incorporate your title, a few benefits, and the audience.

Write this poster board with sound bites that capture attention. Don't be afraid to compare your book with a successful one. For example, it's been said the author's book "WOW! Women of Worth Women Encouraging Women to Purpose and Destiny" is the "Purpose Driven Life" for women.

ACTION STEP:

Write your thirty second 'poster' or 'commercial' for your book. Then practice telling it to a friend until it sounds natural. No friend available? Tell it to an imaginary friend or video tape or use audio to play back and practice.

NOTES

_____

_____

_____

_____

_____

_____

_____

_____

_____

_____

_____

_____

_____

_____

_____

_____

_____

JUMPSTART: TIP 27

It's an adrenaline surge rushing through your body. You have this spark of an idea that keeps threatening to burst into flames and you have to get the words out on paper to match this emotion or picture in your head. After this comes the work of cleaning up the mess that you made. —Janet West

WRITE YOUR BACK COVER BEFORE YOU WRITE YOUR BOOK.

This is ranked the second most important "Passion Point" for your book. Think about it in choosing a book to read for yourself, how many times the title has hooked your interest enough to pick it up.

Then usually you turn it over to see if you really want to read it. On the back cover, you put the most compelling ad copy, benefits, testimonials, and a small blurb (bio) about yourself. If your prospective buyer likes it they will buy instantly. If they need more information to make the decision they will preview your introduction and table of contents.

ACTION STEP:

Write the copy for your back cover. Think benefits and more benefits. Then let your readers know the benefits of getting your book. Pull together some of your best or top testimonials and include as many as you can. Write a short blurb (short paragraph) about yourself. Always write it in second person and in a formal voice.

NOTES

_____

_____

_____

_____

_____

_____

_____

_____

_____

_____

_____

_____

_____

_____

JUMPSTART: TIP 28

Don't use words too big for the subject. Don't say "infinitely" when you mean "very"; otherwise you'll have no words left when you want to talk about something really infinite. —C.S. Lewis

WRITE YOUR BOOK INTRODUCTION.

State the problem your reader has, why you wrote the book, and its purpose. In a few paragraphs include specific benefits and explain your format (how you will present it.)

Make sure it's one page or less. Your sales message will be more subtle here. Nevertheless pinpoint and emphasize the benefits to your reader for you may still be convincing your potential reader your book is the book to buy.

ACTION STEP:

Write a letter to your reader (your book introduction) using the tips above.

NOTES

JUMPSTART: TIP 29

If anything is worth doing, it is worth telling someone how to do it well. --
—Franklin P. Jones

WRITE A TABLE OF CONTENTS.

Each chapter in your table of content should have a sizzling title. If the chapter titles are not obvious, then annotate them. Add some benefits or a sub-title explaining. In "Women's Passion, Purpose & Power," the author put the word "women" in each title. Which creates more synergy? Image, Worth, Name or "A Woman's Image" "A Woman's Worth" "A Woman's Name."

ACTION STEP:

Write a rough draft of your table of contents. Even if you just write a list of questions that you want to answer for your audience, do it now. This will become your table of contents as you work.

NOTES

_____

_____

_____

_____

_____

_____

_____

_____

_____

_____

_____

_____

_____

_____

_____

JUMPSTART: TIP 30

Good order is the foundation of all great things. –Edmund Burke (1729-1797)
British political writer.

USE GOOD ORGANIZATION TO CREATE COMPELLING COPY

Insert graphics that explain not distract. Choose your graphics carefully. They must flow with the theme of your book. Make them further explain your topic. If you choose graphics poorly, they end up distracting your reader. Distracted readers may fall asleep and miss your important message.

Develop pull quotes that summarize. Use pull quotes sparingly but do use them. To make an important point in your chapter, put it in the pull quote. Many times your readers will read the pull quotes first. Then you get to emphasize the point again when they're reading the regular part of the chapter.

Apply white space. Never make your book look like a wall of text. You will frighten lots of readers away and they may never read your message. Most readers start out as skimmers. Your job is to snag their attention with your well organized copy including white space and attention grabbing headlines throughout your book.

ACTION STEP:

If you have your manuscript written, review it for good organization using the tips above. Make any notes for reference later. If you haven't written your manuscript yet, remember to use graphics that help your book explain or tell the story. Sprinkle pull quotes throughout and make sure your copy does not appear as a wall of text.

NOTES

JUMPSTART: TIP 31

If it takes a lot of words to say what you have in mind - give it more thought.
—Dennis Roth

OPEN THE DOOR TO WORLD WIDE OPPORTUNITIES

When your book is ready for purchase, many people will get it from all over the world. With your extended reach, opportunities for you to interact with people outside of your local area will come.

Write a good book; make it easy for your subscribers and customers to tell their friends and associates. Remember, referrals always make the best customers and bring a higher rate of sales.

ACTION STEP:

If not already, find out how to put a Tell-A-Friend script on your book's website. If you are in the planning stage for your book, make a note to tell your webmaster to put a TAF script on book's website. Or find out how to do this yourself.

NOTES

JUMPSTART: TIP 32

The difference between the right word and the almost right word is the difference between lightning and the lightning bug. —Mark Twain

WRITE A BOOK AND GO PLACES YOU'VE NEVER GONE.

At the least, your book will travel to countries and places you've never gone. Better yet, add speaking about your book's topic to your list of services and watch new doors and opportunities for you open. Either way, writing your book will open opportunities to go places you may not get to go any other way.

ACTION STEP:

Even if you are still in the planning stage with your book, <u>begin to consider new services you can add to your business offering</u> that relate to your book. Speaking and Authorship go hand in hand. It's usually a natural progression; people will want to hear what you have to say about your topic because you are an author. Remember, after your book is written you are considered the expert.

NOTES

_____

_____

_____

_____

_____

_____

_____

_____

_____

_____

_____

_____

_____

_____

_____

_____

JUMPSTART: TIP 33

Success demands focus. It is the hallmark of all truly great people. Your ability to get and remain focused or lack thereof is perhaps the key determinant of your success. --Gary Ryan Blair

CREATE MULTIPLE INCOME STREAMS.

Don't just plan a one book event but plan a series of books. It's important to expand your thinking to the possibilities after your book is published. Plan to produce articles, books and updates that help your readers and help you profit from your passion. Each new book or related material will create new profit opportunities, further enhance your visibility and reinforce your credibility as an expert.

Have you thought about your next book? No, really you can start now before you finish your first book, planning for your next For example, when a mentor suggested I do the same exercise below I decided on the tentative series title: Write to Win Series.

ACTION STEP:

Think about it and write possible titles for your two or three book series. Create a title for the whole series and then think about titles for each book.

NOTES

_____

_____

_____

_____

_____

_____

_____

_____

_____

_____

_____

_____

_____

_____

JUMPSTART: TIP 34

Success demands focus. It is the hallmark of all truly great people. Your ability to get and remain focused or lack thereof is perhaps the key determinant of your success. —*Gary Ryan Blair*

CREATE A WRITTEN PLAN.

Do you have your book dream plan written down? Write a [book writing] and even production schedule if you are self publishing. Educate yourself about book writing. Enroll or get resources like e-courses, books and tele-seminars. You can plan to write 1 chapter per week and have a viable short book in 12 weeks. You can have the best plan, intention or goal in the world but chances are you won't accomplish it if it's not written down. So, write it down, get it done and join the elite circle of authors this year.

ACTION STEP:

Write your written plan down on a nice sheet of paper and post it where you can see it daily in your workspace.

NOTES

JUMPSTART: TIP 35

Success is a finished book, a stack of pages each of which is filled with words. If you reach that point, you have won a victory over yourself no less impressive than sailing single-handed around the world. —Tom Clancy

START SMALL

Inexperienced book writers aim too high. Don't try to fit everything you know or researched into a one big book. Plan too big and you may end up with a monster book that turns your potential readers off. Remember many people in the new millennium are busy and impatient. They look for short, quick easy reads.

Solution: Plan a short book first. If you have loads of interesting information, consider breaking your book into parts. Even a series of books is better than one large volume in the non-fiction genre.

ACTION STEP:

Write on the next page your thoughts on the size of your book. Will it be a short book? From the information you have at this moment will you have to divide a monster size book into several books...

NOTES

JUMPSTART: TIP 36

At night, when the objective world has slunk back into its cavern and left dreamers to their own, there come inspirations and capabilities impossible at any less magical and quiet hour. No one knows whether or not he is a writer unless he has tried writing at night. —H. P. Lovecraft

EDUCATE ONESELF ABOUT BOOK WRITING

Many novice book writers fail to educate themselves about book writing. If you've never traveled this road before, enroll in a book writing course. If you have little time, sign up for an email course to jumpstart your writing. Invest in your book project by hiring a professional editor to edit your work.

Solution: Invest time to learn about book writing. A client of mine said, "I want to invest in my work but I have no budget to start with." No worries; more book writers than you know have started with a low to no-string budget. Enroll in free book writing courses. Invest time in learning to self-edit your work until you can afford to hire a professional.

ACTION STEP:

Select <u>step one</u> of a writing program and begin today. Sign-up for twelve lesson online course at http://100daystoabook.com or if getting started is still overwhelming consider the FREE mini-course *Jumpstart Your Book* at http://writetowin.org/jumpstartyourbook.htm

NOTES

_____

_____

_____

_____

_____

_____

_____

_____

_____

_____

_____

_____

_____

_____

JUMPSTART: TIP 37

Words are sacred. They deserve respect. If you get the right ones, in the right order, you can nudge the world a little. —Tom Stoppard

WELCOME TO NEW MILLENNIUM

Work efficiently. Welcome to the new millennium! Remember, don't run from technology; make your software work efficiently for you. Embrace technology. If you don't know how something works, find out. Take a class. Read articles. Learn how to use your software to make things easier and faster. At least take the time to learn about the shortcuts in your current software.

Print out and back up daily. Make a hard copy of your manuscript. Print out changes as you work. Many believe a computer crash could never happen to them. Don't be silly; a computer crash can happen to anyone. Be smart; save your work somewhere besides your computer hard drive. Put it on a floppy disk, flash drive, CD or second hard drive.

ACTION STEP:

Choose the software you would like to know how to use better and sign up for technology class.

NOTES

JUMPSTART: TIP 38

The story I am writing exists, written in absolutely perfect fashion, some place, in the air. All I must do is find it, and copy it. —Jules Renard, "Diary" February 1895

HOW TO TARGET A NICHE MARKET IN YOUR BOOK'S TOPIC AREA:

Identify a problem/solution and research your competition. Then develop a different approach. With all the books in the world on your topic, it's not enough to know the solution. You must present the solution in a different way than existing books do.

Develop a way of making your book different. You need a different viewpoint, a niche, or a different spin on perhaps the same information. Examine the problem again. Look at the solution your book solves with the goal of coming up with a way to present your knowledge differently than existing books.

Here are 3 simple ways to do this:

- **Market Segment.** You can develop a niche by focusing on an occupation, sex, or age group, i.e. Lose 14 Pounds in 2 Weeks: A Guide for Women Above 40, Lose Weight Safely Before, During & After Pregnancy.
- **Focus.** Attack a big problem by emphasizing a particular tool or technique that you have experience with. For example, show how heart attack survivors can lose 14 pounds in 2 weeks by eating only fish, white meats and walking 10 miles a day.
- **Program.** I love this one. Base your solution on the way you solve a large problem by breaking it into steps, i.e. Write Your Best Book Now: An 7 Step Program for book writing.

ACTION STEP:

Identify the top problem and the solution you will present inside your book. Write it in a short paragraph in the note section of this book.

NOTES

JUMPSTART: TIP 39

The world is but a canvas to our imaginations. —*Henry Thoreau*

WRITE A BOOK AND GET PAID HIGHER FEES.

Writing a book elevates you to expert level. You gain instant credibility just by having author behind your name? And that added credibility gives you the power to increase your fees to expert level up to 400% and more.

ACTION STEP:

After writing your book, you are one of the experts in your field. Name three services or products you plan to add to your business related to your book.

NOTES

_____

_____

_____

_____

_____

_____

_____

_____

_____

_____

_____

_____

_____

JUMPSTART: TIP 40

Proofread carefully to see if you any words out. –Author Unknown

PROOFREAD AND LOOK PROFESSIONAL.

Have you read a self published book and noticed misspelled words, a wall of text and grammatical errors? Did it inspire you to read on? Or did it cause you to lose a tiny bit of confidence in the author?

The truth is poor proofreading hurts the self published author and the industry itself. You see, every ounce of confidence lost in one self published author reflects poorly on all independent publishers.

Professionalism inspires confidence. Whether you are writing a short ebook or a full length guide for your industry, your well edited words will work powerfully for you.

In the same way professionalism inspires confidence to purchase your book, grammatical errors and misspelled words may cost you in lost sales. Correct any writing mistakes and translate your professionalism to more book sales.

ACTION STEP:

Do a self-edit on one of your rough draft chapters. Begin to look for a professional editor and/or proofreader for your finished manuscript. Sign up for the *12 Week Book Writing Course* and receive the Self-Editor's checklist as one of the bonus reports at **http://bookwritingcourse.com**

Also, we offer affordable editing packages at *Scribere Creative* **http://scriberecreative.com**

NOTES

JUMPSTART: TIP 41

Never go backward. Attempt, and do it with all your might. Determination is power. —Charles Simmons

AIM TO REWARD YOUR READERS WITH BENEFITS TO THEM.

Write for the 8-10 grade level. Reward your readers with benefits for them. Clear, easy to understand copy makes your reader want to read your piece to the end. Fill your writing with what's in it for them. They'll come back for more and tell all their friends.

Simplifying your writing will help create compelling copy. Include lists, shorter sentences and paragraphs. Slash the passive voice which bogs your reader down. Avoid wordiness; use word pictures and fewer words.

ACTION STEP:

Examine one of your rough draft chapters and look for ways to simplify. Make notes for your self-edit or pass them to your editor.

NOTES

_____

_____

_____

_____

_____

_____

_____

_____

_____

_____

_____

_____

_____

_____

JUMPSTART: TIP 42

Nurture your mind with great thoughts, for you will never go any higher than you think. —*Benjamin Disraeli*

PUSH PAST WRITERS BLOCK!

Do you have writer's block? Don't panic. Here's how to overcome writer's block once and for all. Maintain your momentum keep your writing commitments. Do your ever feel like I am stuck. I have to stop writing until I feel it again.

Don't worry many of us have felt that way. From what I said earlier you may have gotten the impression that you just write when you feel like it and quit when you don't. If so, no that's not what I meant.

Unseasoned writers may play the martyr and push through just to put something on paper or give up and try again another day. We would never get it done like that. When you get stuck simply close that chapter and pull out your chapter outline and choose another chapter.

ACTION STEP:

Print out your table of contents. When you face writer's block pull out your printed TOC and choose another chapter to work on. If you don't have a toc yet, create a simple chapter outline of your book to use.

NOTES

JUMPSTART: TIP 43

I can vividly remember the first sentence I ever wrote in my very first book! It seems like a long time ago. Yet, had I not written that first sentence, I wouldn't have finished that first book, or the second, and so on. And so it goes. Every journey, however long it may be, begins with a single step. But you must take that first step. Once you do, each step takes you closer and closer to your goal.
—*Richard Carlson, Ph.D from Don't Worry, Make Money*

TURN OFF EDITOR MINDSET WHEN WRITING.

Many newbie and seasoned writers are perfectionist. When writing, they feel the urge to stop and change something every few paragraphs. Or they finish a page and want to perfect it before continuing. Turn off your editor voice while writing your first draft. Your goal should be to get the message on paper.

Avoid re-writing during your first draft. After your message is written completely out, then you can turn the editor's voice back up. It's true successful authors rewrite and organize their ideas for the strongest impact. But in the beginning stages of writing your book, concentrate on finishing each chapter.

Use later writing sessions to self-edit. When it's time to edit, check your ideas for flow, grammar, spelling, and chapter endings. Work on your chapter titles and lead in introductions.

ACTION STEP:

Write your first draft manuscript without stopping to edit.

NOTES

JUMPSTART: TIP 44

There are essentially two things that will make you wiser: The books you read and the people you meet. —*Charles Jones*

BUILD A SUPPORT TEAM

Many writers are natural loners. So it's no surprise when they fall into thinking, "I have to do it all myself." Do your research and reading time apart from your writing sessions.

You may be able to ask your spouse, a teen-aged son or daughter, a friend to help with your research. Know when to let go of your chapters and book. Don't self-edit and pick your book apart word by word.

Learn to use your skills at the highest level possible. Some of the mechanical tasks of proofreading ask a family member, part-time employee or again a friend to help. After you have done the best job you can with your manuscript, don't be afraid to pass it to a professional. Learn to delegate faster and faster.

ACTION STEP:

Decide to build a team of support for yourself when writing your book. You might be surprised at who's willing to help. Enlist the help of friends, family, work associates and even professional help. Or you might consider designating one person from your professional support team to assist with your book. Write a tentative list of your support team.

NOTES

JUMPSTART: TIP 45

When I'm writing, I know I'm doing the thing I was born to do. —*Anne Sexton*

FIND YOUR WRITING RHYTHM.

You don't have to write each chapter one after the other. If you get stuck on chapter two, you could be stuck a very long time. This type of thinking comes from grade school where we are ritually taught to do everything in order.

If you have been thinking that way stop right now, no need to raise your hand. You have my permission to work on whatever chapter moves you or you feel passion bubbling for at the moment. Feeling stuck on a chapter, try another. There you have it now go with the flow.

Don't become chained to writing in order. Jump around and fill in the blanks. Review your chapters and whatever subject or topic you most drawn to, begin there.

ACTION STEP:

Write your writing schedule for your book on a sheet of nice paper. Pin it up in your dressing area or where you think you will see it daily.

NOTES

JUMPSTART: TIP 46

The greatest tragedy in life is people with sight but no vision —Helen Keller

WRITE YOUR BOOK'S VISION.

Newbie book writers lose focus and determination because their vision is not clear. When it's not written down distractions easily creep into pull you away your goal of a completed book. You may quickly forget why you are even writing a book.

Can you see your book completed? Take the time to let your imagination run wild in a good way. Envision your completed book and what happens after it's published. Write it down and make it plain. Write when you'll complete it. Name specific outcomes you get after completing your book.

For instance, envision yourself watching your bank balance grow from book sales. Write, "I see myself with increased income and more clients." Anyway you get the idea; create your vision statement including see, hear and feel.

ACTION STEP:

Write your book's vision. Remember write when you'll complete it. Name some specific results you get after it's completed...

NOTES

_____

_____

_____

_____

_____

_____

_____

_____

_____

_____

_____

_____

_____

_____

_____

JUMPSTART: TIP 47

Inspiration exists, but it has to find you working. —*Picasso*

ENVISION WHAT YOUR COMPLETED BOOK WILL DO FOR YOU.

This mistake is similar to writing your book's vision but different because it focuses on the rewards. Many novice book writers fail to dream about the rewards of a completed book. Is your goal to become an expert and gain visibility in your field? Do you want to launch a new career or go to the next level in your current career?

Solution: Fuel the flame of your book dream again. This time dream a bigger dream. Dream after writing your book, you receive life long income that grows each month. You become a highly visible expert in your field. You gain added respect of your colleagues and peers because of your book. You receive increased income leveraged from higher fees charged. Your clients gladly pay them with book author as one of your titles.

ACTION STEP:

Write three to five benefits you will receive after your book is done. Write them down using language as if they have already happened.

NOTES

JUMPSTART: TIP 48

Many aspiring authors tremble in their tracks; they wonder if their book will sell. Good question. No one wants to invest time or money into a sinking ship. Don't be afraid; test your book's significance. —Earma Brown

COUNT YOUR BOOK AS SIGNIFICANT.

Tons of book writers stall at this one. They don't realize the significance of their work. Too easily they think who cares anyway. Why should I add one more book to the 100s of thousands of book already in the world?

Solution: Realize your message is significant and deserves your attention, love and time. Consider what your readers need and want. If your book shares something unique, encouraging, useful, entertaining, it is important enough to be written. Think about your gift? God gave you your gift to share with others. Our gift back to God is what we do with it. The loving care you put into your gift (book) the more rewards await you.

ACTION STEP:

Give your book idea the test of significance.

NOTES

_____

_____

_____

_____

_____

_____

_____

_____

_____

_____

_____

_____

_____

_____

JUMPSTART: TIP 49

Begin to act boldly. The moment one definitely commits oneself, heaven moves in his behalf. —*Gerald R. Ford*

TREAT YOUR BOOK AS A BUSINESS.

It was one thing to write your family's history book. You had no plans of marketing it to the world. It's another thing to write a book about a topic in your field.

Your expectations are different and quite higher. You can expect your book about a topic in your field to brand your business, make you a sought after expert and draw hundreds of new clients.

Set your book up to succeed with a book marketing plan. Your book marketing plan is what I describe as your map. It describes your book, what you will do after the book is completed and published.

It also describes who you hope to sell your book to a target audience. In short you can say your book marketing plan is your roadmap to success and profits.

ACTION STEP:

Create a book marketing plan for your book.

NOTES

JUMPSTART: TIP 50

Nighttime is really the best time to work. All ideas are there to be yours because everyone else is asleep. —Catherine O'Hara

CREATE A SENSE OF URGENCY; NO ONE ELSE WILL!

Many less determined writers get discouraged and quit because their book journey is not as easy and fast as they thought. May I gently say, "Get over it?"

Most worthwhile endeavors take perseverance and hard work. Here's a different perspective; the attention, direction and intent it takes to overcome most obstacles can be developed into new strengths and skills.

Get your book finished now; for now is better than later. Remember you become a successful author the minute you start moving toward your worthwhile book goal. I don't know anyone that regrets they wrote a book. But I know plenty of people that regret they didn't do it sooner.

ACTION STEP:

Select <u>step one</u> of a writing program and begin today. Sign-up for twelve lesson online course at http://100daystoabook.com or if getting started is still overwhelming consider the FREE mini-course *Jumpstart Your Book* at http://writetowin.org/jumpstartyourbook.htm Write your commitment on the next page.

NOTES

JUMPSTART: TIP 51

Success demands focus. It is the hallmark of all truly great people. Your ability to get and remain focused or lack thereof is perhaps the key determinant of your success. —Gary Ryan Blair

BE SPECIFIC.

Avoid generalities. Engage your reader's emotion with specifics. Let them experience color, size and shape. Instead of, "Complete your degree online fast to increase your income." Say, "Complete your master degree online fast so you can upgrade your lifestyle, get vacations, health insurance and other corporate benefits." Specific benefits create a stronger pull than the general benefit of increased income.

ACTION STEP:

Write a short list of specific benefits your reader will receive after reading your book.

NOTES

_____

_____

_____

_____

_____

_____

_____

_____

_____

_____

_____

_____

_____

_____

JUMPSTART: TIP 52

Greater than the tread of mighty armies is an idea whose time has come.
—Victor Hugo

SLASH PASSIVE STRUCTURES.

Passive sentences slow and dull your writing. Get rid of the passive voice sentences. Give your sentences a clear subject and a verb to avoid the passive voice. "The writer found fame and fortune through marketing her books online." instead of "The writer's books were instrumental in leading her to fame and fortune." Avoid connecting verbs like 'was', 'is', 'had', 'that' and 'seemed'. Replace passive voice verbs with active verbs.

ACTION STEP:

Choose your first chapter and check for passive voice sentences. Work on eliminating most if not all passive voice. Visit the resource section for software options for editing help.

NOTES

_____

_____

_____

_____

_____

_____

_____

_____

_____

_____

_____

_____

_____

_____

_____

_____

JUMPSTART: TIP 53

You cannot mandate productivity, you must provide the tools to let people become their best. —Steve Jobs

HOW TO STAMP PRO ON YOUR BOOK

Write attention grabbing chapter titles. Do your chapter titles do their job? I mean do they help explain what's in your book? Do they capture the interest, engage, or shock the senses of your potential reader. Chapter titles set the stage for your potential audience. They work to grab your potential reader by the collar and pull them in for the read.

Craft easily noticed headlines. Add magnetic pulling power and punch to every chapter that will help get your message read. Use your headlines to create excitement, anticipation and enthusiasm for more. Express the heart and passion of your message through your headlines.

Write body copy that aids readability. Aim for short sentences and paragraphs. Slash your sentences to under 15-17 words. Don't bog your readers with complex sentences. Remember multiple phrases slow your reader's comprehension. Make it easy. Get to the point fast.

Use sub-headings and bullets to further organize. Don't forget to use your title writing skill for your chapter sub-headings. Even bullet points will have pulling power if they are developed correctly. Take every opportunity to keep leading your reader along with attention keeping sub-headings and bullets.

ACTION STEP:

Review a chapter for the professional stamp described above. Make corrections and revisions, accordingly.

NOTES

_____

_____

_____

_____

_____

_____

_____

_____

_____

_____

_____

_____

_____

_____

_____

JUMPSTART: TIP 54

An essential aspect of creativity is not being afraid to fail. — *Dr. Edwin Land*

BE PERSISTENT.

Persistent writers become successful authors. Don't give up. Take your dream out of the back seat. Bring your plans to the front. When you do what it takes to author your book, you can reap the rewards – expert status, increased fees, respect for your know how, fame that grows and many more opportunities that manifest.

ACTION STEP:

Think about giving up for no longer than 1 minute. Believe it or not; sometimes it takes the pressure away to at least allow yourself to think about it. But don't do it; don't give up. After thinking about it for a minute or two, then think about some of the rewards you will enjoy when you finish. Visualize (imagine) it in as much detail as you can muster. Now, keep going until you finish.

NOTES

JUMPSTART: TIP 55

A person who can create ideas worthy of note is a person who has learned much from others. —Konosuke Matsushita

WRITE A SIGNIFICANT BOOK.

Many aspiring authors tremble in their tracks; they wonder if their book will sell. Good question. No one wants to invest time or money into a sinking ship.

Don't be afraid; test your book's significance. Your book is significant if it presents useful information, answers important reader questions, and impacts people for the good. If it's entertaining or humorous it could go further than you imagined.

It's significant, if it creates a deeper understanding of humanity, animals or this world. With one to three of these elements your book is worth writing. More than three, it has potential of making great sales —even to best seller status. Go ahead, write your book and make the world a better place.

ACTION STEP:

Which of the qualities above make your book significant? Write them in a short list in the list section.

NOTES

JUMPSTART: TIP 56

It is easier to tone down a wild idea than to think up a new one. —*Alex Osborne*

WRITE YOUR BOOK'S THESIS.

Did you cringe at the word thesis? For some, it brought back memories of English class and writing essays. No worries, a thesis simply reflects the main central thought of the book. Make sure the main central thought includes the greatest benefit of your book and you're done.

In other words, it should answer your audiences' question, "How will this book help, encourage or solve my problem for me?" Writing the thesis before you write the book will keep you on the path of focused, powerful yet easy to read content.

All chapters support your book's main concept. For "Win with the Writer Inside," the thesis is "How to write, complete, and publish your best book fast." The best titles often include the thesis statement in some form.

ACTION STEP:

Write a one sentence thesis for your book.

NOTES

JUMPSTART: TIP 57

If I have seen further it is by standing on the shoulders of giants.
— Isaac Newton

CREATE YOUR BOOK'S WORKING TITLE.

In the literary world it's called a working title because everyone knows it could and probably will change. You may decide to change it or your publisher. Even so, working titles help direct and focus your writing.

Some non-fiction writing does better with subtitles. If needed, it clarifies the title. Confusing titles will miss the mark and sales. Which titles grab you and stir a desire to read what the author has to say: Rich Dad, Poor Dad: What the Rich Teach Their Kids About Money - That the Poor and Middle Class Do Not! or How to Teach Others About Money; How to Win Friends and Influence People! or How to Make Friends.

ACTION STEP:

Create a one to three working titles for your book. Have a contest with your family, Facebook friends or whatever group you feel comfortable doing it. Let them vote on the top title.

NOTES

JUMPSTART: TIP 58

Inspiration could be called inhaling the memory of an act never experienced.
—Ned Rorem

MAKE AN INSPIRATION COVER EARLY.

Keep it by your desk to inspire you. Book covers are the number one selling point of a book. Of course, in the beginning this is only a working cover.

Nevertheless it will help crystallize your thoughts and propel you toward the fulfillment of your dream. Remember, you have about 4-10 seconds to impress your audience to buy.

Browse the bookstores and the internet to get a few ideas. Study the covers best suited for your audience. Choose colors that attract them. Consider blue and red for business books; aqua, yellow, and shades of red work for personal growth books. Avoid using too much red; it makes many feel suspicious.

ACTION STEP:

If you can draw or create graphics on your computer, you can create your own inspiration cover. If not, consider hiring a book cover designer early to bring your creation to life. If that's not an option because of budgetary constraints, you might consider selecting a picture that speaks your message. Visit a free or inexpensive stock photo bank online. I love iStockPhotos.com!

NOTES

JUMPSTART: TIP 59

Change only favours minds that are diligently looking and preparing for discovery. —Louie Pasteur

WRITE THE BACK COVER AS SALES MESSAGE BEFORE YOU WRITE YOUR BOOK.

This benefit driven outline helps give your book direction and helps you focus on what's really important to your readers. Most books will only allow for 50-75 words. That gives you about 8-20 seconds to impress your prospective buyer.

Make this message passionate. Include only what sells: reader and famous testimonials, a benefit driven headline to hook the reader to open the book and read the table of contents, and bulleted benefits.

ACTION STEP:

Go to Amazon.com and find two more back book covers that you like in another field or topic. Examine the sales language and style the writer used. Write a tentative back cover sales message for your book. Remember, write it in second or third person and convince your potential reader this is the book they need to get if interested in your topic. Include a list of benefits the reader will discover inside your book. Use two to three testimonials, if your space permits.

NOTES

_____

_____

_____

_____

_____

_____

_____

_____

_____

_____

_____

_____

_____

JUMPSTART TIP 60

Recognition is everything you write for: it's much more than money. You want your books to be valued. It's the basic aspiration of a serious writer.
—*William Kennedy*

COMPOSE YOUR BOOK'S 60 SECOND "COMMERCIAL" BEFORE YOU BEGIN WRITING.

Have you heard a 60 second radio commercial recently? The information is distilled into sound bytes to be effective. Make your 2-3 sentence book blurbs into a sound byte. Like a radio commercial where you only have a few seconds to get your message across, condense your sound byte into a 60 second tell and sell.

Use your mini commercial at networking meetings, in the elevator, in the grocery line, anywhere you only have a few seconds to tell about your book. Composing your commercial should include your title and three top benefits.

ACTION STEP:

Write a 60 second commercial for your book.

NOTES

JUMPSTART: TIP 61

When we read, we start at the beginning and continue until we reach the end.
When we write, we start in the middle and fight our way out. –Vickie Karp

CREATE AND ORGANIZE YOUR BOOK FILES.

Researchers say we waste over 150 hours a year looking for misplaced information. Create an organization method that fits you. For example, to save time and get organized you can create a master folder with your book's title.

Inside, keep a separate file for each chapter. Assign each chapter a short title that will make sense later. If you don't have a title then assign names by topic.

Put research notes or resources in each chapter named folder. Make a how-to folder as well, such as short-key notes, style or formatting notes. With this system you can manage multiple projects easily.

Stop wasting time with disorganized, unfinished projects that don't produce and help you get your message out in excellence.

ACTION STEP:

Create a simple book file and/or folder to house every piece of information related to your book.

NOTES

_____

_____

_____

_____

_____

_____

_____

_____

_____

_____

_____

_____

_____

JUMPSTART: TIP 62

The greater danger for most of us is not that our aim is too high and we miss it, but that it is too low and we reach it. —*Michelangelo*

MAKE YOUR MARK IN THE WORLD WITH A SIGNIFICANT BOOK.

Many hopeful authors tremble in their tracks wondering if their book will sell. That's a good question. Who wants to invest time or money into a sinking ship? Don't be afraid; here's how to test your book's significance.

You can know your book is significant if it presents useful information, answers important reader questions, and impacts people for the good. If it's entertaining or funny it could go further than you imagined.

It's significant, if it creates a deeper understanding of animals, humanity or this world. With one to three of these elements your book is worth writing. More than three, it has potential of making great sales —even to best seller status. Now, get started; write your book and make the world a better place.

ACTION STEP:

Write a brief paragraph about how your book will benefit your reader.

NOTES

JUMPSTART: TIP 63

It is those who concentrate on but one thing at a time who advance in this world. The great man or woman is the one who never steps outside his or her specialty or foolishly dissipates his or her individuality. —Og Mandino

FIND OUT WHO WILL BUY YOUR BOOK AND SELL IT TO THEM.

When you give your book a specific audience, it will hit the mark of good sales. Best seller books focus on a single topic per book. When you aim at one audience at a time, each tip, each story or how-to will be more effective.

Point your message to someone specific and you gain a competitive edge on many book writers. For many authors just shoot their book out to the world without aim.

It would be helpful to create an audience profile. Are your potential readers male or female? How old are they? Are they interested in topic? What problems do they face? Are they business people or professionals?

Are they techies or non-techies? Are they willing to spend $15-20 on a book like yours? Do this and you're on your way to selling more books than you dreamed.

ACTION STEP:

Who is your target audience? Be specific as you can be. Describe what they look like, gender, age group and economic group.

NOTES

JUMPSTART: TIP 64

I try to leave out the parts that people skip. —*Elmore Leonard*

WRITE DOWN YOUR CHAPTER'S FORMAT.

Readers enjoy easy-to-read maps to guide them through your book. They love consistency. It is disconcerting and unprofessional if you change formats throughout the book.

In non-fiction books, except chapter one each chapter should be similar length and have same sections or categories. To make your chapters come alive, use engagement tools such as anecdotes, your stories, sizzling headings, photos, maps, graphs, exercises, short tips. Readers enjoy easy-to-read side bars in boxes.

ACTION STEP:

Write a simple chapter format for your book.

NOTES

_____

_____

_____

_____

_____

_____

_____

_____

_____

_____

_____

_____

_____

_____

JUMPSTART: TIP 65

Most people have no idea of the giant capacity we can immediately command when we focus all of our resources on mastering a single area of our lives.
—Tony Robbins

WRITE WITH FOCUS.

The biggest blockade for any book writer is lack of focus. You set yourself up for failure if you use the hit and miss approach. You setup your book's framework earlier right? Now transform those sections or table of contents into steps. Make sure your steps flow logically. When I begun work on the book *How to Write Your Best Book Now,* I started with a list of topics. The lists of topics were:

> *Why Write a Book, The Importance of Titles, The Marketing Plan, How to Write Fast, How to Organize Your Book and The Back End of Your Book*

Later, I developed that list of topics into a table of contents with 7 steps clearly defined. It crystallized into a 7 step book writing program. The 7 step program to profit from your passion now looks like this:

> *Design passion points to sell more books, Map Your Journey with a Plan, Sizzle Your Title and Win More Sales, Mine the Gold Called Your Knowledge, Build a successful house for each chapter, Easy Steps to Speed Writing and Create a Winning Streak with Your Book.*

Your audience will reward you by buying your book filled with easy to read step by step instructions to achieve their goal. Now, go ahead focus and transform your list of topics into steps, ways, or solutions to solve your market's worst problem.

ACTION STEP:

Review your table of contents and see if you can turn them into steps. If you have more than 12 steps, try to distill the list down to twelve or less.

NOTES

JUMPSTART: TIP 66

With me poetry has not been a purpose, but a passion. —*Edgar Allan Poe*

KNOW YOUR WHY

Write a book and offer your gift of wisdom about life. Have you been gifted with a deep understanding of life? Put small excerpts of your wisdom throughout your book. Sprinkle your quotes along with other famous philosophers or world thinkers within your book.

Increase your credibility as a service expert. When you write a book, you get instant credibility with your colleagues and customers. They are more willing to work with you and trust you faster with book author as one of your titles. Remember, people tend to buy more and do business with people they trust.

When your book is ready for purchase, many people will get it from all over the world. With your extended reach, opportunities for you to interact with people outside of your local area will come. Write a good book; make it easy for your subscribers and customers to tell their friends and associates. Remember, referrals always make the best customers and bring a higher rate of sales.

ACTION STEP:

Write the significant reasons you are writing a book into an intention statement.

NOTES

JUMPSTART: TIP 67

A little more persistence, a little more effort, and what seemed hopeless failure may turn to glorious success. —*Elbert Hubbard*

KEEP GOING AFTER LIFE INTERRUPTS.

It is a common challenge for book writers to find their place after being interrupted by family, work and daily life. After all that's why many think you must get away to get it done effectively. Yet, there's hope for those who can't get away or choose not to. Successful writers all over the world use the tracking approach. They succeed because they commit to doing a little each day.

Set yourself up for success; use the book tracking approach. The most popular method to use for tracking is time. Time is the method where you commit to a writing a certain amount of time each day.

With the cumulative factor involved your commitment doesn't have to be that much. For example, to accomplish my book writing goals I commit to writing one hour a day in a.m. (my most productive time.) With this method don't be overly concerned about how much you write, just keep the time commitment.

ACTION STEP:

Write out your book writing goals and/or schedule.

NOTES

_____

_____

_____

_____

_____

_____

_____

_____

_____

_____

_____

_____

_____

_____

JUMPSTART: TIP 68

Goals provide the energy source that powers our lives. One of the best ways we can get the most from the energy we have is to focus it. That is what goals can do for us; concentrate our energy. —Denis Waitley

WRITE YOUR PUBLISHING GOALS DOWN.

Will you self-publish or shop for a traditional publisher? There are serious pros and cons for either method. Find out the differences so you can make an educated choice that suits you. If you are self-publishing, consider the POD technology for your book. There are lots of good choices that will publish your book for you at an affordable price.

If you are opting for a traditional publisher, get an agent and a contract before writing the book. Then shop agents and publishers with 2 chapters and a knock-out book proposal. Invest in one of the current writer market guides and research the best fit for your work. It raises your chances considerably if you know what kind of manuscripts a particular company is looking for.

I admit it; getting started writing a book can be challenging to most. Even so, it doesn't have to stay that way. You can do like the author did; use the tips in this book and other experts to kick start writing your book. Start today; complete and release your significant message to the world. Then jump around, get excited for it won't be long before we see your name in print!

ACTION STEP:

Write your publishing plan in short paragraph.

NOTES

_____

_____

_____

_____

_____

_____

_____

_____

_____

_____

_____

_____

_____

_____

JUMPSTART: TIP 69

If you procrastinate when faced with a big difficult problem... break the problem into parts, and handle one part at a time. —Robert Collier

BREAK YOUR WRITING INTO SHORT SECTIONS.

It's easier on you to write, if you break your piece into smaller parts. Furthermore, it's easier on your reader to read. Try to break long paragraphs into shorter, more digestible chunks. Make it easy to read and you'll reach more readers.

Use short sentences and simple words. Writing and reading a long sentence takes longer than a short one. Cut lengthy sentences in half to make your writing easier to read. Aim your copy so a 6-7th grader could understand it. Remember using complex words won't impress your readers. Most times it will annoy them to the point of not finishing your book.

Be concise but specific. Compelling copy is concise. Unnecessary words waste your time and most of all your reader's time. It dilutes your message and makes your book longer than necessary.

Additionally, be specific. When writing your book, stick to the specific information about your topic. The more relevant facts you include, the better. If you don't bother to dig for specifics about your topic, your book may end up vague filled with meaningless words.

ACTION STEP:

Review one to three chapters and chunk (separate) them into parts. Now, put a short title for each part or section. These will become your sub-headings.

NOTES

_____

_____

_____

_____

_____

_____

_____

_____

_____

_____

_____

_____

_____

_____

JUMPSTART: TIP 70

Divide each difficulty into as many parts as is feasible and necessary to resolve it. —Rene Descartes

WRITE WITH PASSION.

Write with all the professionalism you can muster but write from the heart. Write with passion; write with soul. Strategically place your statistics and famous quotes but don't be stuffy with your language. Your readers may think you are talking down to them if you use too many technical terms and professional jargon.

ACTION STEP:

Check your manuscript for stuffy language. Use the right tone to express your message well.

NOTES

JUMPSTART: TIP 71

Every great advance in science has issued from a new audacity of imagination.
—John Dewey

WRITE THE EASY WAY TO FINISH FAST.

Write your book the easy way to finish fast. Five of the top ways to speed write your book includes:

1. *.Act now*. Action will paralyze fear each and every time.
2. *Avoid marathon writing*. Know you don't have to become a hermit to write and complete a successful book.
3. *Commit to the tracking approach*. Doing a set amount —even if it's only 30 minutes to an hour- each day builds a cumulative effect.
4. *Know you don't have to write chapters in order*. You can jump around and fill in the blanks to gain momentum.
5. *Maintain your momentum*. Don't give in to writers block. Move on to work on the chapter you feel passion bubbling for at that moment.

ACTION STEP:

Which one of the speed-writing tips can you commit to using today? Briefly explain; how will you implement it?

NOTES

JUMPSTART: TIP 72

A man should look for what is, and not for what he thinks should be.
—Albert Einstein

OFFER THE MAGIC PILL.

Offer easy solutions to your audience. Offer the magic pill with simple steps to solve a problem in your field. Every one loves it when we get simple solutions to our problems. Get this right and you could have a best seller. Do you know the solution to a vexing problem? Write the solution in your business or self help book. You might be surprised at who's searching for a little relief.

ACTION STEP:

Does your book offer any easy solutions to your audience? Briefly explain.

NOTES

JUMPSTART: TIP 73

Concentrate all your thoughts upon the work at hand. The sun's rays do not burn until brought to a focus. —Alexander Graham Bell

WRITE USING LASER FOCUS.

Apply laser focus to complete your book writing project faster. For example, if you look at a 40 watt bulb, the light is soft. It's not even strong enough to light an average room sufficiently.

Yet you can take the same 40 watts; put it in a laser gun and get a totally different output. In the laser gun, the same 40 watts become a focused beam of light that can cut through different objects like a sharp knife through paper.

Same amount of energy but different focus. To use laser focus in your book project, prioritize, do only one project at a time and complete one project before you start another.

ACTION STEP:

What are your top 3 priorities for this week? Briefly explain, where will your book writing project fit in?

NOTES

_____

_____

_____

_____

_____

_____

_____

_____

_____

_____

_____

_____

_____

_____

_____

JUMPSTART: TIP 74

Bring ideas in and entertain them royally, for one of them may be the king.
—Mark Van Doren

ENTERTAIN YOUR AUDIENCE WITH DRAMA, HUMOR OR FUN.

Yes, I'm still including a non-fiction book in this advice. You can still put bits of drama, humor or fun in your stories, case studies or examples. Enrich the lives of your readers.

Do you have a talent to make people laugh? Use it in your book. Provide a little oasis of escape for your readers. People love it when you entertain them.

Intertwine funny stories into your non-fiction manuscript. Entertain them, make them laugh; they'll love you for it. Best of all, they will have fun telling all their friends about your funny book.

ACTION STEP:

Which element will you use to add interest to your book?

NOTES

JUMPSTART: TIP 75

It's not that I'm so smart; it's just that I stay with problems longer.
—Albert Einstein

OFFER SOLUTIONS TO YOUR AUDIENCE.

Offer simple steps to solve a problem in your field. Every one loves it when we get simple solutions to our problems. Get this right and you could have a best seller in your hands.

Do you know the solution to a distressing problem? Write the solution in your book. You might be surprised at who's searching for a little relief.

You have grown your career, business or service; now write a book to enjoy watching your profits soar to new heights. Then remember stay in touch with your buyers. When they order a book from you follow up with them. Start building your list and send them regular follow-up information, free bonuses and requests.

ACTION STEP:

Write your solution in easy steps.

NOTES

_____

_____

_____

_____

_____

_____

_____

_____

_____

_____

_____

_____

_____

_____

JUMPSTART: TIP 76

I write because something inner and unconscious forces me to. That is the first compulsion. The second is one of ethical and moral duty. I feel responsible to tell stories that inspire readers to consider more deeply who they are.
—David Guterson

PUT ANOTHER STAMP OF PROFESSIONALISM ON YOUR BOOK

Plan to make your manuscript and eventually book the best it can be. Invest in what it takes to make it look and read professional. Don't just get your friends and family to read it for errors; hire an editor. Your editor will not only help you with grammar and spelling but she will help you stay in the same tense. She'll cut all your passive voice sentences that make your book hard to read.

ACTION STEP:

Choose a professional editor to help with your book.

NOTES

JUMPSTART: TIP 77

I think that has to do with my awareness that in a sense we all have a certain measure of responsibility to those who have made it possible for us to take advantage of the opportunities. —Angela Davis

CREATE A GREATER AWARENESS OF YOUR BOOK.

Create a greater awareness of your book and business by offering free articles and tips to your book readers and website visitors. People are always looking for good information, a whopping 85% of Internet users are looking for information.

Make your intent to give something useful and helpful in your area of expertise. As your visitors come for the free, they will become aware of your book and services. They may not buy the first or even the fifth time but expert statistics say up to 50% will buy eventually. Most people purchase something after they've seen it at least 5-7 times.

ACTION STEP:

Select a chapter; examine it to see if you can pull an excerpt out of it and develop into an article.

NOTES

JUMPSTART: TIP 78

The greater danger for most of us is not that our aim is too high and we miss it, but that it is too low and we reach it. —Michelangelo

PUBLISH YOUR PRINT BOOK AS AN E-BOOK.

You will receive your royalties from your original book. But everyone knows you will receive only a few cents on the dollar.

With e-books, you can create and sell directly from your website at full selling price. So as you excerpt portions and repackage your book, always look for ways to develop topics you can sell yourself.

For example, an author has written *7 Steps to Operating a Successful Home Business*. There are several e-book topic directions the author could follow:

- **Market Segments.** The author could direct e-books to specific markets, for example stay-at-home moms who own a home business, successful home business solutions for stay-at-home moms, or for dummies. Still another variant on that target to explore could be ethnicity—African American moms. Another target market could be successful home business solutions for medical professionals.

- **Economic Trends.** The author could consider creating an annual update based on economic conditions, for example home business solutions during a recession, home business solutions when times are tight.

ACTION STEP:

Decide to learn about publishing your book as an ebook. Sign up for a course. Purchase a book and discover ways to add another profit stream for your book. Take notes using the note page inside the book. Consider iWIN's eBook It! ePackage at http://ebookitsuccess.com

NOTES

JUMPSTART: TIP 79

Don't tell fish stories where the people know you; but particularly, don't tell them where they know the fish. —Mark Twain

MAKE YOUR STORIES AND/OR DIALOGUE BELIEVABLE.

Don't make your book read like a long boring speech. It will put your readers to sleep just as a long winded speaker does. Make your short stories reflect real life situations. They will breathe life into your book and keep the reader reading.

Inspire people to do something good. Weave inspiring stories into your book and sell more. The *21 Irrefutable Laws of Leadership* spent 18 straight months on the Business Week Business Best Seller List. Dr. Maxwell started each chapter with a short story of a famous person successfully using the chapter's law of leadership.

ACTION STEP:

Select one of your chapters and examine it to see if you can add a short inspirational but related story. Perhaps you can add it in your introduction, closing summary or as a spotlight.

NOTES

JUMPSTART: TIP 80

Details create the big picture. —Sanford I. Weill

WRITE COMPELLING COPY

Cut selfish constructions containing 'I'. Minimize the "I" in your writing. Your audience wants to know what you can do them. Answer their questions. Solve their problems with each solution. During the editing process, circle each "I" and replace as many as you can with a "you" centered sentence.

Avoid pompous language. The shortest, most well known words are best. The more syllables in a word, the less compelling it becomes. Cut all unnecessary adjectives.

Slash adverbs. Go through and cut words like openly, suddenly, very that tell the reader instead of show the reader. Circle all the –ly and very words. Pull out your thesaurus and replace them with power words that show emotion or describe.

ACTION STEP:

Self-edit what you have written so far and implement the compelling copy tips above.

NOTES

JUMPSTART: TIP 81

Energy and persistence conquer all things. —*Benjamin Franklin*

FILL IN THE WEAK SPOTS OF YOUR EXISTING KNOWLEDGE WITH RESEARCH.

As you begin to uncover your nuggets and chunks of knowledge related to your central idea or concept you will uncover areas where you are missing supporting information. Now is the time to locate it. The starting point for research is your local library, bookstore and the Internet. Guard against plagiarizing the work of others, but identify areas you need to explore further to gain facts and ideas that support your book's theme.

Avid readers make the best writers. If not already, develop or strengthen your habit of reading. For your book writing project, begin to analyze what you read. Look for books that relate to your topic and read them. Take note of the ones you like the best. Analyze what made them easy to read or what set them apart from the others. Also, take note of any new ideas you come across.

Mining the gold called *your knowledge* starts by recognizing that you probably already possess most of the information you need to complete your unique book. Using the principles of organizing and prioritizing it outlined in this chapter, you will quickly have the bare bones of your book in hand. By analyzing your background and observations to the core ideas and organizing them, you will write and complete your book faster than ever dreamed.

ACTION STEP:

Decide what book you will read in the next 30 days. If you are already reading, considering adding one more book to your list in the next 30 days.

NOTES

JUMPSTART: TIP 82

Success is almost totally dependent upon drive and persistence. The extra energy required to make another effort or try another approach is the secret of winning. —Denis Waitley

TURN THE EDITOR MINDSET BACK ON.

Professionalism inspires confidence. Whether you are writing a short ebook or a full length guide for your industry, your well edited words will work powerfully for you.

In the same way professionalism inspires confidence to purchase your book, grammatical errors and misspelled words may cost you in lost sales. Correct these writing mistakes and translate your professionalism to more book sales.

Start well. Create a sizzling start. Hook your readers through emotion. Slant your book or introduction with a question or an amazing statistic. Share the top benefits of your book early. Target the 'You' in every reader.

Shorten your introduction. Entice your reader with the main benefit (main central thought) early to keep them reading. Write the rest of your piece to support your main central thought. Sprinkle the rest of the benefits throughout your copy in descending priority.

ACTION STEP:

Go through and examine each chapter and make sure you start well. Did you start with a question to prompt interest or an outstanding statistic? Either one will give you a good start.

NOTES

JUMPSTART: TIP 83

Nothing in this world can take the place of persistence. Talent will not; nothing is more common than unsuccessful people with talent. Genius will not; unrewarded genius is almost a proverb. Education will not; the world is full of educated failures. Persistence and determination alone are omnipotent.
—*Calvin Coolidge*

WRITE COMPELLING COPY II

Check for endings and beginnings. Make sure each chapter has a clear beginning and an ending. All other sections within chapter should have a clear transition to another section.

Appeal to the senses of sight, sound and emotions. Showing is more effective than telling. Instead of "Buy this product today because it's profitable," say, "Would you like to double, even quadruple your business income in five months?

Write for a specific audience. Let's face it; not everyone will enjoy your book. There's even some that are totally NOT interested in your book's topic. So, you should write for the readers who are interested in your topic. Select an audience that loves your topic and write a book for them.

ACTION STEP:

Self-edit what you have written so far and implement the compelling copy tips above.

NOTES

JUMPSTART: TIP 84

As long as we are persistence in our pursuit of our deepest destiny, we will continue to grow. We cannot choose the day or time when we will fully bloom. It happens in its own time. —Denis Waitley

WRITE COMPELLING COPY III

Are you ready to translate your professionalism to profits? Check for and correct the below mistakes and watch your sales soar from the minute you publish. Remember to develop a sizzling start, shorten your introduction, slash the passive voice, shorten sentences, write compelling copy, avoid generalities and slash the adverbs.

Search for ly. Use action and not adverbs. Omit words that end with (ly) like suddenly or quickly. If your sentence loses impact, look for better verb. Show action and emotion. The (ly) words are usually unnecessary. They also will slow your reader's pace.

Check for clarity. Read a paragraph for understanding. This is a good task to assign to a family member or an assistant. Instruct them to circle the paragraphs that are not clear.

Check for run-on paragraphs. You can shorten sentences and paragraphs. Look for the start of a new thought. Connecting words like also and then can usually break into a new paragraph. Careful, don't put a paragraph break in the middle of a thought. Make sure it flows naturally.

ACTION STEP:

Self-edit what you have written so far and implement the compelling copy tips above.

NOTES

JUMPSTART: TIP 85

Ambition is the path to success. Persistence is the vehicle you arrive in.
—Bill Bradley

HOW TO GAIN MOMENTUM.

Completing your first book will build your confidence. I know short doesn't mean the same thing to every person. For books, let's agree 50-100 or so pages is short, even 140 sounds less intimidating than a 200-300 page book.

Your future customers are busy and usually read only what takes the shortest amount of time. For example, a colleague of mine wanted to learn how to conduct tele-seminars. He said he didn't hesitate buying a short book of 70 pages at $19.97 to help him learn the ropes of tele-seminars.

ACTION STEP:

If your first book manuscript is more than 200 pages, determine if you can shorten it.

NOTES

JUMPSTART: TIP 86

I write because something inner and unconscious forces me to. That is the first compulsion. The second is one of ethical and moral duty. I feel responsible to tell stories that inspire readers to consider more deeply who they are.
—David Guterson

HOW TO MAKE YOUR BOOK HARD TO PUT DOWN

Even if your book is non-fiction, fill it with anecdotes, short stories and case studies. Don't make it read like a boring speech. If it puts your readers to sleep; they may put it down and never pick it up again. Create short stories that reflect real life situations. Your readers will love it and tell all their friends and family about your interesting book. The stories will breathe life into your book and keep your readers reading to the end.

ACTION STEP:

Decide if you can put stories in your chapters.

NOTES

JUMPSTART: TIP 87

If you really want something you can figure out how to make it happen. —*Cher*

REACH MORE PEOPLE.

I know you are passionate about your topic. You have volumes of information. But if you can do this, your work will not suffer. Here's what I'm talking about; slash your BIG book in half. Too many aspiring writers overwhelm themselves with goals of a 365 page book first.

Shorten your book to 25-90 pages the first time or divide your large book into a smaller book one and two. Though you shorten it, still fill it with useful information by using the question and answer format for each chapter. Using the same format and length for each chapter and answering all your readers' questions will not only speed your writing process but it will result in a successful book.

ACTION STEP:

If your book is big, how can you shorten it?

NOTES

JUMPSTART: TIP 88

Every great dream begins with a dreamer. Always remember, you have within you the strength, the patience, and the passion to reach for the stars to change the world. — Harriet Tubman

GO TO MARKET FASTER AND PROFIT SOONER.

In this case, short is good. Write a short to do two things. If your book is shorter and easier to write fast, you can expect to go to market sooner. To speed up your writing time, write your book in chunks, chapters, sections and parts.

Writing this way will allow you to refine, repeat and repackage your information. Develop a continuing flow with a website, a stream of articles, reports, follow-up products and even services to build your book, your brand and your profits further.

ACTION STEP:

Examine your manuscript; can you see obvious sections and parts? Go through and put sub-headings over each part.

NOTES

JUMPSTART: TIP 89

Nothing great in the world has ever been accomplished without passion.
— Georg Wilhelm Friedrich Hegel

CREATE A SYSTEM.

The process of checking your background for ideas should be continuous. As you write your book, you will find yourself continuing the process of organizing and re-organizing your ideas. Take your list of ideas and add any nuggets you located while reviewing your background, speeches and articles.

As you progress, new ideas will come to you. It's o.k. to jot your ideas down on a piece of paper until you have a chance to file it. But for some of us, our desk can quickly become a hodge-podge of sticky notes and scraps of paper. Now is the time to create your system that you will use throughout writing your book. Judy Cullins puts it like this, "Stop Piling and Start Filing."

Research experts say over 150 hours a year is wasted looking for misplaced paper. Organization is key because the Pareto Time Management says that only 10% of our papers are actually important.

I suggest creating a hard copy file and computer file version for your book. I realize some may favor the hard copy and some may favor the computer system. Ultimately, I don't think it matters that much which one you choose as long as you setup a system that works for you.

For the hard copy version of your book files, make one vertical or hanging folder for your book. Then take one manila folder for each chapter and label it with chapter's shortened name. Take one manila folder for each part of your book: front matter, back matter and even promotion or marketing folder. When you give each part of your book a place in your book file, you will find it fast and write your book fast.

ACTION STEP: Create a system of steps to write your book faster. List simple steps in your book writing plan and schedule.

NOTES

_____

_____

_____

_____

_____

_____

_____

_____

_____

_____

_____

_____

_____

_____

JUMPSTART: TIP 90

What is now proved was once only imagined. — *William Blake*

RE-EXAMINE THE FILES FULL OF YOUR WRITING AND SPEAKING.

Even if you are not published yet, you probably have a lot more knowledge stored that you have written or created than you realize. As a professional, you have written memos, proposals and reports.

You may have conducted meetings, delivered presentations and speeches or short talks. These may all contain valuable information which you have forgotten. Gather any and all information you have collected over the years into one place.

ACTION STEP:

Make a list and write down the title or topic of every article, proposal, report or presentation that you have ever given. Next to the topic or title write down the main idea that you developed in them.

Then skim the actual report, speech or article and look for relevant nuggets of information that you can re-use. Dissect each piece for ideas that should be added to your book topic.

NOTES

JUMPSTART: TIP 91

When you come to a roadblock, take a detour. — *Mary Kay Ash*

PLAN HOW YOUR BOOK WILL BE PUBLISHED.

Whether you choose self-publishing or a traditional publisher, there are pros and cons to either method of publishing your book. If you choose to pursue a traditional publisher for your book, you should know your book proposal is a sales (direct-marketing) document with a sole purpose.

It's single purpose is to convince a publisher that your book will earn a profit, if published. The proposal should focus on the size and buying power of the targeted market you will attract, the problem your book solves, how your book plans to solve the problem, how different your book is from others already published on the subject and how you plan to promote your book.

ACTION STEP:

Write a short one page book proposal. Need more help with writing a one-page book proposal? Visit *http://butterflypress.net* the Butterfly Press Online Book Store. Or sign up for the 12 Week Book Writing Course **http://bookwritingcourse.com** and receive this bonus report inside the course.

NOTES

JUMPSTART: TIP 92

If one dream should fall and break into a thousand pieces, never be afraid to pick one of those pieces up and begin again. —Flavia Weedn

MAKE IT EASY TO REPACKAGE; CHUNK IT.

Write your first book in chunks, chapters, sections and parts. Writing this way will make your manuscript easy to refine, repeat and repackage after your book is published. Develop a website, a stream of articles, reports, follow-up products and even services to build your second book, your brand and your profits further.

ACTION STEP:

Decide what product you will develop from your book's information first after your book is published.

NOTES

JUMPSTART: TIP 93

No matter how old you get, if you can keep the desire to be creative, you're keeping the man-child alive. —*John Cassavetesn*

EMBRACE YOUR AUDIENCE IN YOUR PLAN.

Yes, it's true; not everyone will be interested in reading your book. Even so, I'm convinced there's a community of people in your field waiting for you to solve their problem. What problems does your message solve for them? Develop an audience profile (picture) and keep it in front of you as you write. That way you can visualize a real person to solve problems for.

Additionally, knowing your market before you write will help you write focused, compelling chapters. Writing to a specific person or group of people will keep your readers reading to the end. Write too general and your readers may put your book down and never pick it back up to finish.

ACTION STEP:

Choose the person or group you will write your book to as a target audience.

NOTES

JUMPSTART: TIP 94

No idea is so outlandish that it should not be considered with a searching but at the same time steady eye. — *Winston Churchill*

CREATE MORE WITH YOUR INFORMATION.

Create additional exposure for your book with informational reports. Most of the time people are online looking for free information. Your report may consist of a single idea, an expansion of an idea or a brief overview of the contents you cover in a chapter. Consider writing a column using your information as a starting point. You could tie in with current events and your opinion. Columns interpret more than educate. They permit you to give your opinion on current trends, events or outside influences affecting your readers.

ACTION STEP:

Examine your book manuscript and look for possible report topics. You can plan to elaborate on a subject lightly covered in your book. Or you might consider spotlighting a specific topic in your report from your book.

NOTES

_____

_____

_____

_____

_____

_____

_____

_____

_____

_____

_____

_____

_____

_____

JUMPSTART: TIP 95

We have to understand that the world can only be grasped by action, not by contemplation. The hand is more important than the eye... The hand is the cutting edge of the mind. —Jacob Bronowski

CONTINUE TO BUILD AWARENESS

Continue to plan activities and events that bring attention to your book indirectly. One simple step is to put your book's title and subtitle in your email signature. The more exposure you and your website receive the more your credibility builds to support you as an expert and author in your field.

ACTION STEP:

Make a list of events and activities you plan to conduct during your book writing phase or after your book is written.

NOTES

JUMPSTART: TIP 96

The profit of great ideas comes when you turn them into reality.
—Tom Hopkins

USE YOUR BOOK INFORMATION TO CREATE MORE

Develop newsletters, columns, courses based on the information gathered for your book. Email newsletters offer you another opportunity to keep in touch with your readers. Your newsletters can be either informational or opinionated. Either way, they give you an opportunity to remain visible and build even more credibility.

Compile your book's case studies and testimonials. Your case studies and testimonials further promote your book, competent service, or product. The testimonials and even case studies speak up for you. Everyone is more open to something that someone else has tried first.

ACTION STEP:

Make a list of possible spin-off articles and information products you can create from your book information.

NOTES

_____

_____

_____

_____

_____

_____

_____

_____

_____

_____

_____

_____

_____

_____

_____

JUMPSTART: TIP 97

Writing a book is an adventure. To begin with, it is a toy and an amusement; then it becomes a mistress, and then it becomes a master, and then a tyrant. The last phase is that just as you are about to be reconciled to your servitude, you kill the monster, and fling him out to the public. —*Winston Churchill*

CREATE A WONDERFUL WEB SITE

Develop your website. If you don't have one that focuses on your book or you as an individual, create one. Your website is now one of the first places agents, publishers and clients will look to find out more about you.

The better quality it is, the more it will pre-sell your book proposal or your book itself. First impressions are important. Make your website a good one that accurately reflects you as an individual.

ACTION STEP:

Take three easy steps to get started on your web site. Select a short domain name, purchase hosting and develop website to upload to server. Sounds like techno jumbo? Hire a web site developer or use popular web site builder software to get your web site ready. If you are a do-it-yourselfer like the author, you may be looking for more information about developing a website yourself. Go to this website for more information:

http://clickeasywebsites.com

NOTES

_____

_____

_____

_____

_____

_____

_____

_____

_____

_____

_____

_____

_____

_____

JUMPSTART: TIP 98

Trust yourself. You know more than you think you do. —*Benjamin Spock*

YOU KNOW MORE THAN YOU THINK.

You have gained a certain level of success in your field, career or even hobby. You may be an active consultant, business owner, speaker, or writer. In your field you have been constantly learning and observing. On your path to success through failures, successes and opportunities to learn, you have been accumulating the information you need to complete your book.

You have experienced and observed what works and does not work. You have developed over time an understanding of what order things should happen and how it appears out of order when it doesn't happen in that order. Through the process of continually doing what you do, you have gained a wealth of knowledge and information.

The challenge is that your knowledge is unorganized. Once you create a structure for organizing your ideas, your ability to create your book and/or books will quickly take shape.

ACTION STEP:

If not already, begin to gather all your chunks and groups of information into one place.

NOTES

JUMPSTART: TIP 99

Nothing is particularly hard if you divide it into small jobs. —*Henry Ford*

DIVIDE AND CONQUER.

Begin to break your knowledge into chunks of information. The beginning point is to begin separate your files, speeches, articles into general topics. For example, I have bodies of information for my inspirational writing and a whole other body or topic for business writing.

And of course there's another topic for the how-tos of writing in my files. When I first started, I went through and separated these chunks of information into different folders and eventually as my chunks of information grew I had to house them in separate file units.

After creating topical groups, break your knowledge for your book into individual ideas or chunks of information so you can inventory what you already know on the subject.

You'll notice as you organize and inventory the ideas you already possess; it will uncover some areas that your knowledge is bit weak. Once you identify the weak areas in your knowledge, it becomes easy to locate the information needed to fill in the gap or strengthen the weak area.

ACTION STEP:

After gathering your existing information into one place, organize it into file and file folders labeled by chapters.

NOTES

_____

_____

_____

_____

_____

_____

_____

_____

_____

_____

_____

_____

_____

_____

JUMPSTART: TIP 100

*Divide each difficulty into as many parts as is feasible
and necessary to resolve it. —Rene Descartes*

INCLUDE THE EDITOR'S CUT IN YOUR PLAN.

Give yourself a break. You don't have to write a 350 page book like your colleague to be successful. It doesn't even have to be 150 pages. Simply write a short book approximately 100 pages long and fill it with your insightful information, your expertise and/or your experiences.

You get to shorten your examples and stories. With a short book, you have no pressure to add every piece of information you know about your topic. Instead, if you have too much information simply divide your material into two books. Your readers will love you for it. They'll buy both books because they are easy to read and short.

ACTION STEP:

Be brutal; take your huge manuscript and cut. Make everything shorter, punchier and to the point.

NOTES

JUMPSTART: TIP 101

Every great dream begins with a dreamer. Always remember, you have within you the strength, the patience, and the passion to reach for the stars to change the world. —Harriet Tubman

PURSUE YOUR MOST PASSIONATE IDEA.

For now, put aside your list of topics. Take a break and relax. Remember, successful books are based on one central idea. The author concentrates on one main theme to drive their book to success. Textbooks can get away with a list of all kinds of facts. But non-fiction books, especially how-to books are based on one main idea.

The central idea provides the focus needed to make your writing compelling. For your book, you need a viewpoint, a position, and a conclusion that you develop fact by fact or step by step as you write your book.

Readers look for an easy read. They look for a book that will help them solve their problem step by step. They need interpretation, perspective and sequence.

The easiest way to come up with a main idea for your book is to follow your passion. To choose a subject that you will be still be passionate about in a year or so, ask yourself these questions:

What ideas am I really passionate about, What ideas do I consistently discuss no matter where I am? What ideas do I really want to share with the world? Where do I see others making the same mistakes I did? How can I help people with my knowledge? What key ideas helped me succeed or caused me to fail? What main idea can make a difference in the lives of others?

The main idea for your book may come to you when you least expect it. So over the next few days begin to mull it over in your mind. Spend some quiet time, if only for a few minutes during the day to think about your deep passion, your mission, the idea that really moves you.

This is important because if you pinpoint your passion well, the easier it will be to write a book that expresses what you want to express.

ACTION STEP: Select your most passionate topic to form into a book.

NOTES

_____

_____

_____

_____

_____

_____

_____

_____

_____

_____

_____

_____

_____

_____

JUMPSTART: TIP 102

Imagination is the living power and prime agent of all human perception.
—Samuel Taylor Coleridge

MAKE A COMMITMENT.

It takes a commitment to write a book and especially if you want to write it fast. Make your commitment and write it down. If you don't write it down, you may lose the fortitude to finish. *Gerald Ford* said it like this, "Begin to act boldly. The moment one definitely commits oneself, heaven moves in his behalf."

ACTION STEP:

Write out a simple one to three sentence commitment to write your book in the next 100 days.

NOTES

ABOUT AUTHOR

Earma Brown lives in Northern Texas with husband Varn. She is an author, publisher and book coach strategist who teaches entrepreneurs, teachers, coaches and infopreneurs how to put their core message into a saleable book. Earma has a Bachelor's degree in Business. Author of twelve books, Earma's expertise has been shared in five writing helps books and hundreds of expert articles. Using her signature *Write to Win* products and *iWIN* programs, Earma's clients learn how to transform their original works into multiple products and services.

WHAT'S NEXT?

SIGN UP FOR 100 DAYS TO A BOOK COURSE
12 Week Book Writing Course

Uncover the best way to get your wildly successful book written fast! For all the details on a proven program that walks you through 12 amazingly simple lessons to get your BEST book written and out to the world. Now is better than later:

1. Online 12 Week Book Writing Course with Bonus Reports
http://www.bookwritingcourse.com

2. How to Write a Book in 100 Days companion workbook (paperback)
http://www.butterflypress.net/store/

JOIN IWIN MEMBERSHIP & COMMUNITY

Are you ready to discover how use YOUR information to write books, create products and grow your own profit stream. Discover how to tap into your inner creativity, create connection with other writers and build community!

http://writersinformationnetwork.com | http://iwinontheweb.com

BOOK WRITING AND PUBLISHING RESOURCES

Information & Resource Website
http://bookwritinghelp.com
Book Writing Coach Blog
http://writetowin.org

BOOK PUBLISHING
http://butterflypress.net
http://selfpublishinghouse.net
http://selfpublishyourbooknow.com

AUTHOR SERVICES, BOOK COVER DESIGN, BOOK TRAILERS
http://scriberecreative.com

Free Ezine
http://writetowin.org/jumpstartyourbook.com

OTHER BOOK WRITING & SELF PUBLISHING BOOKS:

Write Your Best Book Now
100 Exciting Reasons to Write a Book
Writing a Book God's Way
Self Publishing Your Way Now

BOOK ORDER INFORMATION

Butterfly Press Books
P.O. Box 180141
Dallas, Texas 75218
http://butterflypress.net/store/

NOTES

_____

_____

_____

_____

_____

_____

_____

_____

_____

_____

_____

NOTES

www.ingramcontent.com/pod-product-compliance
Lightning Source LLC
Chambersburg PA
CBHW080048280326
41934CB00014B/3248